Animal Mothers

Animal Mothers, by Atsushi Komori, illustrated by
Masayuki Yabuuchi. Text copyright © 1983 by
Atsushi Komori. Illustrations copyright © 1983
Masayuki Yabuuchi. Reprinted by permission of
the Putnam & Grosset Group.

Houghton Mifflin Edition, 1996
Copyright © 1996 by Houghton Mifflin Company.
All rights reserved.

Printed in the U.S.A.

ISBN: 0-395-75261-2

123456789-B-99 98 97 96 95

Animal Mothers

Atsushi Komori

Illustrated by Masayuki Yabuuchi

HOUGHTON MIFFLIN COMPANY

BOSTON

ATLANTA   DALLAS   GENEVA, ILLINOIS   PALO ALTO   PRINCETON

Mother cat carries her kittens
in her soft mouth.

Mother lion carries her cub in her mouth, too.

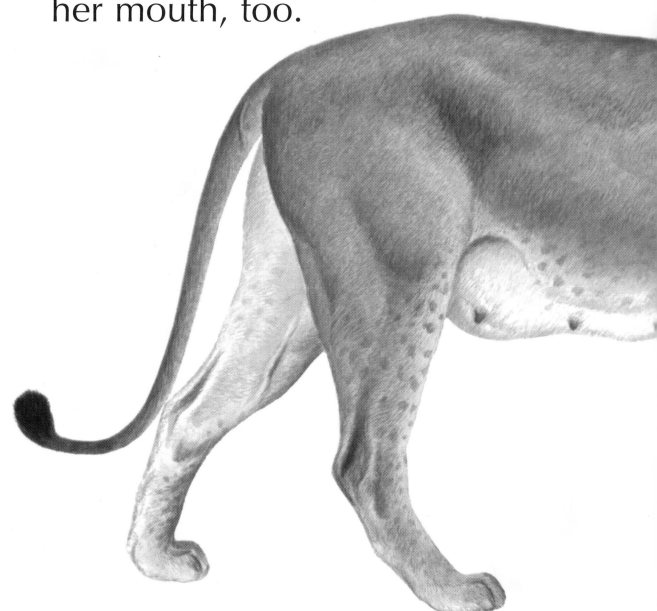

Mother baboon's baby clings tightly to her stomach.

Mother chimpanzee carries
her baby in her arms.

Mother koala's cub
rides on her back.

Mother sloth carries her baby on her stomach.

Mother kangaroo carries
her joey in her pouch.

18

Mother elephant gently pushes her baby with her trunk to make it run.

The zebra foal runs along behind its mother.

Baby wild boars follow their mother all in a bunch.

Baby hedgehogs follow their mother in a nice straight line.